GAME CHANGER

For Lewis and Henry —J.C.

To my wonderful and patient wife and our equally wonderful and patient boys, all my love —R.D.

Text copyright © 2015 by John Coy
Illustrations copyright © 2015 by Randy DuBurke

Carolrhoda Books
A division of Lerner Publishing Group, Inc.
241 First Avenue North
Minneapolis, MN 55401 USA

For reading levels and more information, look up this title at www.lernerbooks.com.

Illustration of Texas Western's 1966 NCAA Championship team based on a photo from the University of Texas at El Paso.

Main body text set in Typo American Com 15/20.
Typeface provided by Linotype AG.

Library of Congress Cataloging-in-Publication Data

Coy, John, 1958–
      Game changer : John Mclendon and the secret game / by John Coy ; illustrated by Randy DuBurke.
        pages cm
      Includes bibliographical references and index.
      ISBN 978-1-4677-2604-7 (lb : alk. paper)
      ISBN 978-1-4677-8810-6 (eb pdf : alk. paper)
      1. McLendon, John B. 2. Basketball coaches—United States. 3. African American basketball coaches. 4. Discrimination in sports—United States. 5. North Carolina College for Negroes 6. Duke University—Basketball—History. I. Title.
      GV884.M29C69 2015
      796.32307'7—dc23   2015000910

Manufactured in the United States of America
1 - DP - 7/15/15

GAME CHANGER

JOHN McLENDON AND THE SECRET GAME

John Coy

2015

ILLUSTRATED BY

RANDY DuBURKE

CAROLRHODA BOOKS MINNEAPOLIS

Who are you?

What are you?

Why are you here on
this earth?

Where are
you going?

—Coach John McLendon's four questions for his players

On Sunday, March 12, 1944, at eleven in the morning, when most people were still at church, a group of basketball players who thought they were the best in the state of North Carolina piled into two cars.

The members of the Duke University Medical
School team knew they were playing a game,
but they didn't all know where they were
going or who their opponent would be.

The drivers wound around the deserted streets of downtown Durham to make sure nobody was following them. Before they crossed over to the other side of town, the players covered the windows with quilts so they wouldn't be seen.

When the cars stopped, the players
pulled their coats over their heads
and walked through the women's
locker room into a gymnasium.

Before them stood a timekeeper, two referees, and the starting five of the North Carolina College of Negroes. The Eagles, under their young coach John McLendon, had nineteen wins and one loss, but because of segregation, they were prohibited from playing against white teams. On this day, the Eagles were going to break that prohibition.

Coach McLendon, who'd learned basketball from James Naismith, the game's founder, stood to the side with his wife, Alice, and their two children. McLendon believed basketball could change people's prejudices, and he wanted his children present to see just such a change.

The two teams warmed up at opposite ends of the locked gymnasium. Players glanced down to size one another up and then turned away. Eventually, there was nothing left to do but play ball.

The game started slowly, with dropped
passes and shots clanging off the rim.

Players on both
sides, some of whom
had never been this
close to a person of a
different color, were
hesitant to touch or
bump into one another.

The Duke team of Jack Burgess, Dick Symmonds, Homer Sieber, Dave Hubbell, and Dick Thislethwaite took the lead. They had all played college ball and were strong and experienced. They ran their three-man weave, executed give and goes, and launched set shots.

This was the game as most people knew it—basketball of the present.

The young Eagles gradually settled into their game, though. They applied the pressure defense they'd learned from Coach McLendon. George Parks and Henry "Big Dog" Thomas grabbed rebounds and fired outlet passes to Aubrey Stanley, Floyd "Cootie" Brown, and James "Boogie-Woogie" Hardy. They raced up and down the floor in McLendon's innovative fast-break style that emphasized attacking the basket.

This was basketball the white players had never seen.

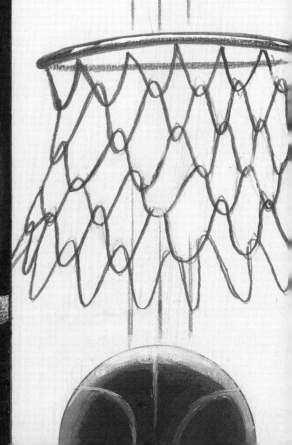

The Duke players breathed hard and grabbed their shorts. They'd never imagined the game at this pace. As they gasped for breath, the Eagles, who were in excellent condition because of McLendon's drills, made basket after basket.

The Duke players were witnessing something new—basketball of the future.

When the game ended, the players were shocked by the score. The Duke team had scored forty-four points, which was near its average. The Eagles, though, had eighty-eight, doubling Duke's score. It was a stunning display of basketball.

There was no question about which team was the best. "They beat us real good. They beat us real sharp," Jack Burgess said.

What happened next was even more remarkable.

The two teams played another game,
but this time, black and white players
played together to even up the sides in
a game of shirts and skins.

Meanwhile, word spread
around campus that
something was happening at
the gym. Students climbed
up on window ledges and
pressed against the glass
to see a sight they'd
never seen.

Nineteen years before Dr. King's "I Have a
Dream" speech and three years before Jackie
Robinson broke the color line in Major League
Baseball, black players and white players
worked together as teammates in an illegal game
in segregated North Carolina.

George Parks of the Eagles said later that
this game was "just God's children horsing
around with a basketball."

Afterward, the Eagles' players invited the Duke players back to their dormitory. They sat around and talked about the game and everything else—the way basketball players do.

When it was time for the Duke players to go, everybody agreed on a plan. They pledged they would keep the game secret to protect one another and Coach McLendon, who would have been fired or much worse if people found out.

A reporter for the *Carolina Times*, Durham's black weekly newspaper, heard about the game, but he agreed not to publish the story at McLendon's request since the Ku Klux Klan was active and considered "race mixing" a crime punishable by death.

Jack Burgess did write a letter to his family in Montana. "We played basketball against a Negro college team. . . . We sure had fun and I especially had a good time, for most of the fellows playing with me were Southerners. . . . And when the evening was over, most of them had changed their views quite a lot."

These players had seen the future, but it would take time for everybody else to see it.

Twenty-two years later, in 1966, Texas Western started
five black players against a heavily favored, all-white
team from Kentucky for the national championship.
Texas Western triumphed, and when they did, news spread
around the country. The era of segregated big-time
college basketball was ending.

Years later, John McLendon, who was inducted into the Basketball Hall of Fame for his pioneering coaching career, said, "I just wanted to further the idea that we all played basketball, that we all played it well, and that we should be playing it together."

Today, people don't think twice about players of different skin colors competing with one another on the court, but it wasn't always that way. It took courage to make that future a reality. Coach John McLendon and those brave players who rose to the challenge in the Secret Game were years ahead of their time.

AUTHOR'S NOTE

John McLendon (1915—1999), whose mother was Delaware Indian and whose father was African American, studied under James Naismith, basketball's inventor, at the University of Kansas. He went on to a position at the North Carolina College of Negroes, where he became head basketball coach in 1940 and revolutionized the game.

Later, at Tennessee State, McLendon became the first coach ever to win three consecutive national titles (1957 to 1959). He was the first black coach in the American Basketball Association, the first at a predominantly white school, and the first black coach inducted into the Naismith Memorial Basketball Hall of Fame. Throughout his life, John McLendon was a game changer.

Thank you to Scott Ellsworth for shining a light on this story; Milton S. Katz, for his excellent biography; and Coach McLendon and the men who participated in the Secret Game for sharing it with us.

TIMELINE

1863   The Emancipation Proclamation is issued.

1944   The Secret Game is played.

1947   Jackie Robinson integrates Major League Baseball.

1950   Nat Clifton, Chuck Cooper, and Earl Lloyd integrate the NBA.

1954   Brown vs. Board of Education dismisses "separate but equal."

1963   Martin Luther King Jr. gives his "I Have a Dream" speech.

Mississippi State plays the integrated Loyola University team in the NCAA basketball tournament after having previously boycotted the tournament in protest of integration.

1964   The Civil Rights Act is passed.

1966   Texas Western defeats all-white Kentucky in the NCAA basketball championship game with an all-black starting five.

SELECTED BIBLIOGRAPHY

Black Magic. DVD, Directed by Dan Klores. Narrated by Samuel L. Jackson. Produced by Dan Klores, Earl Monroe, Libby Geist and David Zieff. Bristol, CT: ESPN Films, 2008.

Ellsworth, Scott. "Sunday March 31, 1996: JIM CROW LOSSES; the Secret Game." *New York Times Magazine*, March 31, 1996. http://www.nytimes.com/1996/03/31/magazine/sunday-march-31 -1996-jim-crow-losses-the-secret-game.html

Katz, Milton, *Breaking Through: John McLendon, Basketball Legend and Civil Rights Pioneer.* Fayetteville: University of Arkansas Press, 2007.

McLendon, John B. *Fast Break Basketball: Fundamentals and Fine Points.* West Nyack, NY: Parker, 1965.